ASTROLOGY

SAGITTARIUS

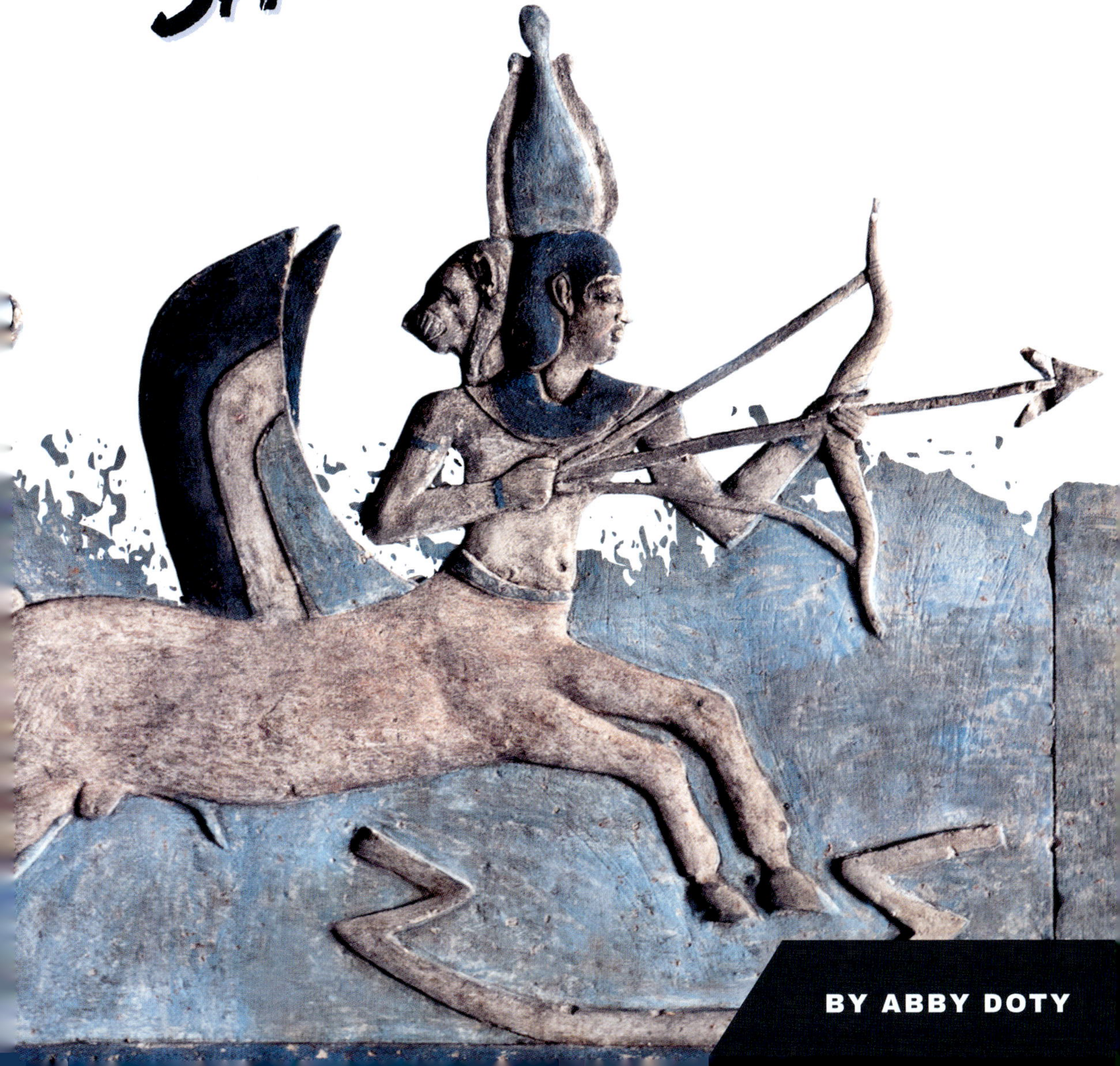

BY ABBY DOTY

Apex is distributed by North Star Editions:
sales@northstareditions.com | 888-417-0195

Produced for Apex by Red Line Editorial.

Photographs ©: Shutterstock Images, cover (illustration, constellation), cover (background), 1, 4–5, 6–7, 12–13, 14, 16–17, 18, 20, 21, 22–23, 24, 25, 26–27, 29; iStockphoto, 8, 10–11, 19; Werner Forman/Universal Images Group/Getty Images, 9

Library of Congress Control Number: 2025939154

ISBN
979-8-89250-788-2 (hardcover)
979-8-89250-817-9 (paperback)
979-8-89250-874-2 (ebook pdf)
979-8-89250-846-9 (hosted ebook)

Printed in the United States of America
Mankato, MN
012026

NOTE TO PARENTS AND EDUCATORS

Apex books are designed to build literacy skills in striving readers. Exciting, high-interest content attracts and holds readers' attention. The text is carefully leveled to allow students to achieve success quickly. Additional features, such as bolded glossary words for difficult terms, help build comprehension.

TABLE OF CONTENTS

CHAPTER 1

THE ARCHER

Sagittarius is a **constellation**. Its name is Latin for "archer." People say the stars show a bow and arrow. An archer is shooting it.

Sagittarius is one of the biggest constellations in the night sky.

People have told many stories about this constellation. Some said the archer was a **centaur**. Others thought he was a satyr. Satyrs are half human and half goat.

Art in some Egyptian temples shows centaurs and other figures based on constellations.

CROTUS

One Greek **myth** said the constellation was a satyr named Crotus. He invented the hunting bow. He also played music. When Crotus died, the god Zeus placed him in the stars.

Scorpius appears near Sagittarius in the night sky.

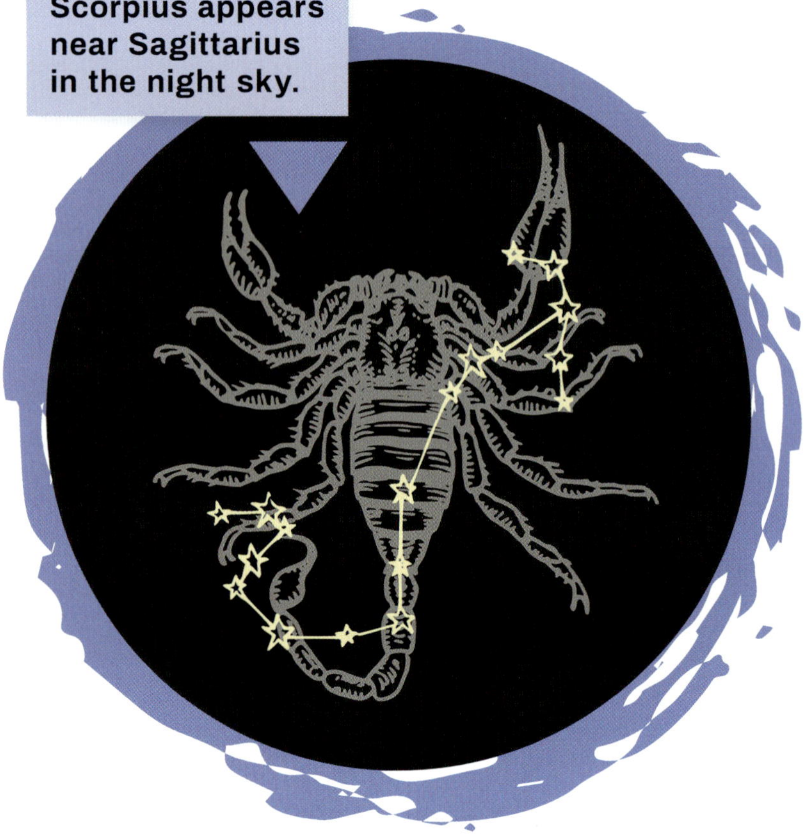

In the night sky, Sagittarius's arrow points toward Scorpius. That is another constellation. It looks like a scorpion. One Greek myth said the archer attacked it.

FAST FACT

In Babylon, some people linked Sagittarius with the god Nergal.

Nergal (right) was described as a god of death and war.

CHAPTER 2

THE ZODIAC

Sagittarius is part of the **zodiac**. There are 12 zodiac signs. They split the year into 12 parts. Sagittarius is the ninth sign.

The signs of the zodiac are often shown in a wheel.

Sagittarius's time begins around November 22. It ends around December 21. People born during this time have Sagittarius as their **sun sign**. They are called Sagittarians.

GO WITH THE FLOW

Sagittarius is a mutable sign. That means it comes at the end of a season. A shift between seasons often brings changes. And people with mutable signs are said to be **flexible**.

Sagittarius's time comes as fall turns to winter in northern parts of the world.

In astrology, sun signs are thought to shape people's **personalities**. For example, Sagittarians are said to love adventure. They like to travel and try new things.

FAST FACT

Sagittarians are often described as funny and playful.

Sagittarians may enjoy thrill rides and other exciting activities.

CHAPTER 3

ABOUT SAGITTARIUS

Like all zodiac signs, Sagittarius has a **glyph**. It is an arrow with a line through it. It represents the archer's bow and arrow.

Each zodiac sign is paired with a glyph and a constellation.

Jupiter is the biggest planet in the solar system. In astrology, it is linked to luck and wisdom.

In astrology, ruling planets are said to shape how people act. Sagittarius's ruling planet is Jupiter. This planet has ties to growth. And Sagittarians often push limits and have big ideas.

In Roman myths, Jupiter was the king of the gods.

FAST FACT

Many Sagittarians are very busy. They always want to do more.

Each sign is matched with an element. The elements are water, fire, earth, and air. Sagittarius's element is fire. Fire signs often have lots of energy.

Like flames of fire, Sagittarians often leap from one thing to the next.

According to astrology, water signs feel things deeply. So, they may not always get along well with fire signs.

GETTING ALONG

Astrology says that fire signs tend to speak and act quickly. They get along well with air signs, who also think fast. But they can make earth signs feel nervous. And they can hurt water signs' feelings.

CHAPTER 4

MANY INTERESTS

Sagittarians are known for being social. They often have lots of friends. They love going out and doing things with others. And their bright personalities draw people in.

Many Sagittarians are good at helping other people have fun.

Taylor Swift is a Sagittarian. She has released music in several different styles throughout her career.

Sagittarians are also curious. They love to learn and grow. And they're not afraid to try new things.

SHARING STORIES

Many Sagittarians are creative. They tend to be good storytellers as well. Several famous Sagittarians fit these traits. One is Taylor Swift. Billie Eilish is another.

Billie Eilish is known for using unusual sounds in her music.

Sagittarians can sometimes be messy.

Sagittarians often have many interests. They may have trouble finishing things or keeping promises. They may need to practice staying focused and seeing things through.

FAST FACT

Sagittarians are known for being very honest.

COMPREHENSION QUESTIONS

Write your answers on a separate piece of paper.

1. Write a few sentences explaining the main ideas of Chapter 4.

2. Do you enjoy trying new things? Why or why not?

3. What element is Sagittarius matched with?

- **A.** fire
- **B.** earth
- **C.** water

4. According to astrology, what is something a Sagittarian might struggle with?

- **A.** learning something new
- **B.** doing the same thing every day
- **C.** making new friends

5. What does **social** mean in this book?

*Sagittarians are known for being **social**. They often have lots of friends.*

- **A.** trying to spend time alone
- **B.** liking to be with others
- **C.** having a hard time making friends

6. What does **curious** mean in this book?

*Sagittarians are also **curious**. They love to learn and grow.*

- **A.** wanting to know less
- **B.** wanting to stay at home
- **C.** wanting to know more

Answer key on page 32.

GLOSSARY

centaur

A creature with the upper body of a human and the lower body of a horse.

constellation

A group of stars that form a shape.

flexible

Willing to make changes and try new things.

glyph

A shape that stands for a word or idea.

myth

A well-known story from the past that often includes magic.

personalities

The ways that people usually act.

sun sign

A person's main zodiac sign, which is decided by the date they were born.

zodiac

The set of 12 signs used in astrology, based on a part of the sky that the sun appears to move through each year.

TO LEARN MORE

BOOKS

Betts, Bruce. *Jupiter: The Largest Planet*. Lerner Publications, 2025.

Goldstein, Margaret J. *Mysteries of Stars*. Lerner Publications, 2021.

Loh-Hagan, Virginia. *Star Signs*. Cherry Lake Publishing, 2021.

ONLINE RESOURCES

Visit **www.apexeditions.com** to find links and resources related to this title.

ABOUT THE AUTHOR

Abby Doty is a writer, editor, and booklover from Minnesota. Her sun sign is Aquarius.

INDEX

ANSWER KEY:
1. Answers will vary; 2. Answers will vary; 3. A; 4. B; 5. B; 6. C